ACTIVATING YOUR SPIRITUAL SENSES

THE EMPOWERMENT SERIES

Kingdom infusion books that empower you to live
on earth as it is in heaven

Books in the Empowerment series by Jerame Nelson:

Activating your Spiritual Senses

Activating the Justice of God

Activating your Dream Language

Activating God's Power in Your Life

ACTIVATING YOUR SPIRITUAL SENSES

A closer look at having
a supernatural relationship with God

Jerame Nelson

Living at His Feet Publications
Living At His Feet Ministries
591 Telegraph Canyon Rd. Suite 705
Chula Vista, CA 91910

www.livingathisfeet.org
admin@livingathisfeet.org

ISBN   978-0-9849687-1-8

For Worldwide Distribution, Printed in the U.S.A.
1 2 3 4 5 6 7 8 9 10 11 / 09 08 07 06

Cover design by Brian Blount: www.webvisiongraphics.com
Page design by Mark Buschgens: www.markedbydesign.net

CONTENTS

FORWARD

While I was reading this book I began to think about the famous Helen Keller who was born mute, blind, and deaf. Her family hired a teacher named Annie Sullivan, who believed that Helen was intelligent and worthy. Annie taught Helen sign language in her hands over and over, but it took quite a process before Helen understood her first way of communicating. She had none of her natural senses to rely on except for touch and smell; but these are not normal communication senses in the way we commonly think of them. This repetition of handing Helen a doll and signing it in her hand over and over, or giving her water then signing that as well, took a while before Helen had her break through moment. But when it did, it opened up her whole world to understanding.

Helen learned so fast and began to have huge ideas about the world around her. She couldn't see it through her eyes, but she could see it through her heart. She couldn't hear it through her ears but she had an inner dialogue with God that helped her to listen. She couldn't speak through her voice but she was a spokeswoman for a generation of people and revealed principles that only one who had a deeply awakened inner self could know. She taught us all that you don't need natural senses but your spiritual ones are imperative.

She shared this through being extremely vulnerable and putting her life and weakness on display. As a result, she became a historical figure who is still celebrated today because she did not allow herself to be held back by her limitations. She taught us that humanity is not bound to their natural senses, but to their spiritual ones. This is exactly what she meant when she said:

"I can see, and that is why I can be happy, in what you call the dark, but which to me is golden. I can see a God-made world, not a manmade world."

And: "It is a terrible thing to see and have no vision".

She was the ultimate picture of a woman of faith who leaned into the presence of God and developed the marvelous gift of spiritual senses and was considered one of the greatest humanitarian and spiritual thinkers of all time.

This book is going to help you awaken your five spiritual senses in the same way that Helen Keller went on a journey to have hers develop. You are never limited when you go on this developmental journey to mature in your spiritual senses. They are what bridge the gap between just having intellectual knowledge and actually understanding and believing in what we know.

Obviously, for every natural principle there is a spiritual counterpart. I know you will not only enjoy the incredibly faith-building stories that are included in these pages but even more, it will build a foundation in you for the rest of your life.

God is maturing the body of Christ at large so quickly through the Holy Spirit revealing God's nature to us. There is no quicker way to adapt to this nature then to experience it by relationship to our spiritual senses. When Jesus was on the earth there were so many ways that God revealed Himself in and through Jesus, it wasn't just intellectual knowledge but it was through His voice, His touch, His breath.

The culture of heaven that Jesus represented is living and active and can be felt, seen, heard, tasted, and smelled spiritually - it is real. Even though you are already a part of this heavenly reality when you get saved, only through allowing your spiritual senses to be awakened and developed will you be able to experience the fullest measure this side of eternity. We don't have to live with just knowledge, we can, through our spiritual senses, have experiences that will draw these scriptural truths into the deepest fabric of our beings.

I have known Jerame for years and watched him operate in exactly what he details in this book. I love that he is able to give such clear language to the spiritual senses that makes it easy to grasp how God is not just limited to speech when he interacts with us - just like we don't communicate or relate to the world around us in the natural by one sense alone. Jerame gives us an ability to see and feel, to taste and smell the very nature of God. Its time to believe for John 10:10 the **Abundantly full life**, which I will apply in context to this book as this: We need to be open to have a full sensual experience that we might fully understand the Christ who is dwelling within us and the atmosphere that this dwelling causes around us.

Have fun reading this book and take seriously what you learn. Apply it to your life and I guarantee you will feel a deeper connection to the God you love so much.

Shawn Bolz
Senior Pastor of Expression58 in Los Angeles, California
Author of *The Throne Room Company,*
Keys to Heaven's Economy,
& The Nonreligious Guide to Dating and Being Single

ACTIVATING YOUR SPIRITUAL SENSES

A closer look at having
a supernatural relationship with God

The Bible is very clear about the fact that we were all created with both natural and spiritual senses. This book will demystify some of the things of the supernatural and give you a framework so that you can begin to fully experience God in your life and enter into the gift of discernment. This book will also open up your understanding through God's word, as well as through some of my personal experiences with God, so that you can become more sensitive to the Holy Spirit's leading in your life. Along the way, the Holy Spirit will speak to you, impart revelation and knowledge of the ways of God and draw you closer.

Just like we have been created to experience the world we live in with the 5 natural senses of taste, touch, sound, sight, and smell, so too, we have we been created to experience God with those same senses in the spirit realm. The Word reveals that exercising our spiritual senses is necessary to increase in the gift of discernment.

Hebrews 5:14 gives us a glimpse into mature believers exercising their spiritual senses to discern good from evil: *But solid food is for the mature, who because of practice have their senses trained to discern good and evil.* (NAS)

This shows us how every human was created by God to experience things in the natural realm as well as the spiritual. It is for you to see, hear, touch, taste and smell in the natural and in the spirit. For the things of the spirit cannot be discerned only in the natural. We need our "spirit man" to come alive and interact on an entirely different sensory level. Then, we can discern good and evil around us, discern the spiritual entities in the environment, and understand the motivations and intentions of others. We can also tune into the many aspects of God's presence – sense the angelic, smell His fragrance, see in the Spirit, taste His goodness, hear the thoughts of God and discern the thoughts of others, and feel His presence increasing in your life.

ACTIVATING YOUR SPIRITUAL SENSE OF HEARING

The first of the 5 senses I would like to talk about is the sense of hearing or sound. The Bible is full of stories were God opens the sense of sound in the spirit to people.

In Genesis 3:8-9 you see the first account of God opening up the sense of hearing in the spirit to a human as Adam heard the sound of God walking in the garden. *They heard the sound of the LORD God walking in the garden in the cool of the day, and the man and his wife hid themselves from the presence of the LORD God among the trees of the garden. Then the LORD God called to the man, and said to him, "Where are you?"*

Then in 1 Samuel, we see God opening young Samuel's ears to hear the audible voice of God but it took awhile for the boy to discern that God was speaking. He could hear, but he didn't know who was talking.

So the LORD called Samuel again for the third time. And he arose and went to Eli and said, "Here I am, for you called me." Then Eli discerned that the LORD was calling the boy. And Eli said to Samuel, "Go lie down, and it shall be if He calls you, that you shall say, 'Speak, LORD, for Your servant is listening.' " So Samuel went and lay down in his place. Then the LORD came and stood and called as at other times, "Samuel! Samuel!" And Samuel said, "Speak, for Your servant is listening."

You also see in the New Testament that Jesus, along with many others, heard the audible voice of God when Jesus' cousin John baptized him in the river Jordan. Matthew 3:16-17 tells us that when Jesus was baptized the heavens opened and God the Father spoke audibly. *After being baptized, Jesus came up immediately from the water; and behold, the heavens were opened, and he saw the Spirit of God descending as a dove and lighting on Him, and behold, a voice out of the heavens said, "This is My beloved Son, in whom I am well-pleased."*

Many who were standing by that day heard the sound of God speaking in their spirit. However, not all heard the voice. Some accounts of scripture tell us that some heard the voice of God and others heard what appeared to be as lightning and thunder. This shows us that some people are more in tune to hearing through their spirit then others.

God wants us to hear in the spirit. He longs to open your ears to hear the sounds from heaven and the sounds in heaven.

I remember one time while doing a tent revival meeting in

Florida, the Lord opened up our ears to hear the sound of the angels praising God. There were around 6,000 hungry worshipers in this huge tent lifting up praises to God. At one point in the worship the crowd began to scream and shout at the top of their lungs for around 30 minuets. Then, all of a sudden, we all began to hear the most beautiful sound of singing. The crazy thing was that the singing sounded like no singing we had ever heard before. It was like a beautiful symphony of voices all singing in perfect harmony. Everyone knew the angels were singing. There was only one girl who was leading worship yet it was as if hundreds of people were singing in perfect harmony above the stage. It was amazing. The sound came down from on top of us and broke into the meeting as we were all shouting and praising God.

This was one of the first times that God had opened my ears to hear the sounds of heaven.

Another time I was in Atlanta, Georgia speaking at a series of meetings. Before the first night of the meetings, I went to the pastor's house for dinner. As we were eating with his whole family and talking, we were all interrupted by the sound of a loud trumpet blast over our heads. It was awesome yet shocking at the same time. There was no one else home that night and no one had a trumpet. It was totally supernatural. God had opened our ears to hear in the spirit what was going on in the heavens.

Later that evening, as I prayed about the meaning of this sign, the Lord spoke to me out of the book of Revelation and showed me that the trumpet sound represented the voice of the Lord. In Revelation 1:10, John heard the sound of the Lord's voice and it sounds like a trumpet blast. He wrote, *I was in the Spirit on the Lord's day, and I heard behind me a loud voice like the sound of a trumpet…*

He then went on to tell me that our assignment was to release the voice of the Lord prophetically in that region that weekend.

Signs and wonders can come in many different ways but always point to something. In the book of Acts, chapter 2 tells us that on the day of Pentecost everyone was gathered together in one accord praying in an upper room, and suddenly they all heard the sound of a mighty rushing wind come into the room. Then, tongues of fire appeared over their heads they were all filled with the Holy Spirit and began to speak in tongues. God opened their spiritual sense of hearing that day. The Bible says that there was a sound of a mighty rushing wind. It didn't say that there was a mighty rushing wind that came into the room that day. It said there was a **sound** of a mighty rushing wind. They heard the **sound** of what God was releasing in the spirit then experienced it in the natural (see Acts 2:2).

Whenever we have true encounters with heaven, fruit always follows.

I remember sitting on the front row of this church that I used to be on staff with in Abbotsford BC, waiting on God to see if He would speak to me. As I positioned my self to be still before God to hear His voice, suddenly God opened up my sense of hearing in the spirit and I heard the sound of a gemstone fall and hit the ground. At that time we had been seeing gemstones manifesting quite often in meetings. So after I came out of this encounter, I leaned over to our main Pastor and whispered in his ear that I had just heard the sound of a gemstone fall in the spirit, and that I thought that God was going to release one in that set of meetings that we were doing. So I told him to agree with me for a gemstone to manifest from heaven. That night, as the offering was being taken, a women dropped her pen while making out a check and found a 2 1/2 karat diamond from God on the floor next to her pen. The next day the women had three different appraisers look at the stone and all three said it was a perfect diamond and appraised it at over $30,000 dollars.

Have you ever heard the sound of God? It can be powerful or it can be subtle. He speaks with Words audibly or to your spirit where only you can hear Him. He rushes in with a sound of wind or He releases a sound that is of particular significance only to you, a sound that only you would pick up on and immediately know its meaning. Did you ever hear your name called when no one was around you? Did you know enough to say, "Speak God, your servant is listening?" Have you ever heard the sound of gemstones falling or rain? Ask God to open your spiritual sense of hearing. And get ready for what comes next.

An empowerment prayer to get you there:

Lord open up to me the sense of sound in the spirit that I might know you more, and hear your voice more clearly in my spirit. Also, open up my ears to hear the sounds of heaven. The things that no ear has heard or mind conceived, let me hear them so that I might walk that much closer to your heart, in Jesus' name.

ACTIVATING YOUR SPIRITUAL SENSE OF TOUCH

Now I want to talk to you about the sense of touch. God wants to open up your sense of touch in the spirit so that you can tangibly feel His presence in order to know Him more as well as partner with Him to do the works of His kingdom here on the earth. Have you ever wondered why some people are more sensitive to the Spirit of God then others? Or why some people seem to manifest in the Holy Spirit like crazy and others don't feel a thing? This is a huge question that many are wondering about in the church today. In fact, for quite a few years, I often wondered about this as well. Then, as God began to unveil this revelation of the five senses of the Spirit to me, I began to understand why this was so. One of your five senses in the natural is touch or feel. This is one of the main ways we function as human beings. We are sensitive to both good and bad feelings and have learned how to live our lives according to the sense of touch. We have learned what to do and what not to do because of this sense being activated in our lives.

There are many examples in the Bible of people who felt the presence of God.

Jesus was sensitive to the touch of the anointing of God in his life. One of the ways He was able to minister so effectively was that he was sensitive to the feeling or sensation of the power of God as the Holy Spirit flowed through Him to touch people's lives. In Mark 5:25-34 the Bible tells the story of the healing of the women with the issue of blood. Let's take a look at this story and you will see that not only was Jesus sensitive to the release of the anointing of God, but so was the women who was healed.

Now a certain woman had a flow of blood for 12 years. 26 and had suffered many things from many physicians. She had spent all that she had and was no better, but rather grew worse. When she heard about Jesus, she came behind Him in the crowd and touched His garment. For she said, "If only I may touch His clothes, I shall be made well."

Immediately the fountain of her blood was dried up, and she felt in her body that she was healed of the affliction. And Jesus, immediately knowing in Himself that power had gone out of Him, turned around in the crowd and said, "Who touched My clothes?"

But His disciples said to Him, "You see the multitudes thronging you, and you say, 'Who touched me?'" And He looked around to see her who had done this thing. But the woman, fearing and trembling, knowing what had happened to her, came and fell down before Him and told Him the whole truth.

And He said to her, "Daughter, your faith has made you well. Go in peace, and be healed of your affliction."

This is an amazing example of God opening up the sense of touch in the Spirit in the life and ministry of Jesus, as well as with the woman with the issue of blood. This scripture shows us that Jesus was so sensitive to the Holy Spirit that He felt, or immediately knew, that the anointing had gone out from Him when the woman with the issue of blood had touched him. This took place in a large crowded area - probably a market place were hundreds or thousands were all gathered together in a city square to buy food or do business. In the midst of this crowded place and this woman touching Jesus, He was able to stop immediately and discern that power had left His body. As this happens His disciples think he is crazy as He cries out, "Who touched me? They say to him, "You see the multitudes thronging you, and you say, 'Who touched me?'"

God wants to open up the sense of touch so that He can minister to you in such a way that you know beyond a doubt that He touched you. The first thing that happens to the woman with the issue of blood is that ***she feels the touch of God heal her*** and it leads to not only her miracle but to her salvation. After she feels the blood immediately dry up she comes trembling under the presence of God to Jesus. And when He sees her, He declares to the women that she is now a daughter of God and to go her way because her faith had made her well.

I believe the number one reason why God wants to open up

our senses in the Spirit is so that we would know Him more - especially through the sense of touch and feeling. David cried out in the Psalms for God to open up his ability to feel God's presence. He said that his heart and flesh cried out for the living God (see Psalms 84:2). I believe that God wants to encounter us with His manifest presence. We need to be changed, expanded, in our ability to feel His presence.

In 2 Chronicles 5:13-14 it says that as the house of Israel lifted up high praises unto The Lord and the result was that a cloud of glory came into the room carrying the presence of God so heavy that the priest could not stand to minister as a result of the intensity of God's glory. I believe there are times when God wants to overwhelm us with His presence and change who we are just like the priest we were just talking about and the woman with the issue of blood whose life was changed forever. They were changed just because of one encounter. The priest could not stand. The woman was healed. And they knew the touch of God and the power of God.

I remember early in my walk with the Lord one of the first times the Lord encountered me through the sense of touch. It was an encounter that changed everything for me. At the time I was living in Abbotsford BC, and was hanging out with a friend who had had way more experiences in the supernatural then me. At this point in my life I had not really had any angelic encounters before. I was desperate to encounter God and had been praying for the supernatural gifts of God's Spirit to be activated in my life daily.

My friend ended up telling me about this time that an angel had encountered him and imparted to him a gift of revelation. He went on to tell me that when the angel had visited him he noticed that the angel was holding a gift in its hand. Then as he noticed this, the angel walked up to him and shoved the gift into his belly. Afterwards, the Holy Spirit spoke to him and told him that a gift of revelation was just imparted to him that day. After this visitation He began to have a lot of visionary experiences with God. After he told me about this encounter that he had had with the Lord he went on to prophesy over me about how God wanted to encounter me like He did with him. Then he went on to tell me to expect to receive an encounter soon.

So I went home and was super excited to press into the Lord. That night, I began to press in through worship and prayer but nothing really significant happened. The next day at around 6:30 a.m., I got up to pray again. As I began to pray in tongues, in a mater of a few minutes, I fell into a trance and entered into an encounter with the Lord. As I did everything went blank - but all of a sudden I could sense that there was an angel in the room and then, all of a sudden, **boom**, I felt a hand go in my belly and the presence of God overwhelmed me.

Then, I came out of the trance and was shocked about the visitation. After I came out of this encounter, I began to ask God about the meaning of the experience. The Lord went on to tell me that I had just had an encounter like my friend told me about and that He had just sent an angel to impart to me a gift to see in the spirit. After God spoke this to me,

I was excited! Just like my friend had prophesied, I had received an encounter with an angel and God had given me a gift of revelation. I began to realize that the encounter for me was totally different then my friend's experience. He saw the angel but I did not. In fact, I didn't see anything at all, but I could feel the encounter happening. I could feel the presence of God and the angel's hand as he shoved the gift of revelation into me and that was it. I didn't see anything.

I learned something powerful that day about encountering God. Even though I didn't see the angel like my friend did and only sensed and felt the encounter happen. The results were still the same. Just like my friend, I had received an impartation to **see in the spirit**. Dreams and visions took off to a whole new level after that point. The only difference was that the Holy Spirit decided to open up my **sense of touch** rather then my sense of sight in the spirit. I learned that day that it was all about fruit and results. There will always be ongoing fruit when we really encounter heaven. From that day on, I began to experience a major increase of visionary encounters from the Lord that involved both touch and sight.

Some Christians might think that it's more spiritual to see things in the spirit rather then to hear them but the reality is that one is not better then the other. In scripture, God uses both sight and feelings to speak. The most important thing is receiving clearly the message or impartation that the Lord wants to give you.

The reality is that we are all wired differently. We all have different gift mixes and strengths in our ability to hear from God and one is not better then the other - they are just different. What God wants is for us to become childlike and learn how He speaks to us. In my own walk with the Lord, I do have dreams and visions at times, but the majority of the time God speaks to me in the still small voice or through a feeling or an impression. I have learned to have just as much faith in the still small voice of the Lord as I have when I have a vision or a dream. In fact often times I find it easier to understand what God is communicating to me through hearing the still small voice of God, or a feeling or impression in the spirit, then I do when I have a dream or vision. This is because often times a dream or vision requires an interpretation. A lot of times it can take hours, days, or even weeks of prayer to clearly understand a vision or dream. In fact, in my meetings while ministering words of knowledge for healing, I would almost rather have the Holy Spirit speak to me through the sense of touch, feeling, or the still small voice of the Lord rather then in visions. The reason why is because it's usually a more clear and accurate word when I feel or hear because I don't have to interpret the vision right there on the spot in front of the people I'm ministering to.

I love when the Holy Spirit opens the sense of touch to me in healing meetings! It makes things easy. If I feel a sudden pain in my back that I know is not mine I will simply just call out a word of knowledge in the meeting and tell people that God showed me that someone needs a miracle in there back and if they respond to the word they will get healed. It's that easy.

God wants to highlight things to us by activating our spiritual senses. Often, after I will feel pain in my body that I know is not my own and is a word of knowledge for someone else, I will ask God questions. Let's take the situation of feeling someone's back pain from the above example, for instance. After God highlights the back pain I will often ask him questions like *what is wrong with this person's back?* Then the Holy Spirit might speak to me and say *two slipped disks*. Then I will take what I have felt and combine it with what I have heard and it makes for a powerful word of knowledge, which then sparks the faith of the person I am calling out to be healed. Then the result is the miracle. This is a great example of how God wants to activate our spiritual senses so that we can partner with him to do His work on the earth. You may not be a preacher like me who holds regular healing meetings every week, but we all come into contact with people in everyday life. God wants to open up your sense of touch so that you can get accurate words of knowledge and partner with Him to minister to people in everyday life just like Jesus did with the women with the issue of blood.

Next time you feel a sudden pain in your body that doesn't seem normal to you, ask the Holy Spirit if it's a word of knowledge for someone else around you to get healed. Then as the spirit leads you, step out and ask people if they have the pain you are feeling. It will spark faith in the person you are praying for as well as in your own life when you step out to be used by God. Almost 95% of the time I feel the condition and step out in the streets to pray for healing, the person is healed. Began to ask God to open your sense of touch to get words of knowledge for people as you go about every day life. Then watch how God uses you!

Have you ever felt the touch of God come on you power-fully so that you could not stand in His presence? Or felt His healing hand release power that cured you of some illness or pain? Do you know what it is like to feel His presence, receive His anointing, and step out to touch another and feel His presence flow through you? There is so much more for you. Ask God to activate your spiritual sense of touch.

An empowerment prayer to get you there:

Lord, I pray that you would open up my sense of touch in the spirit; that I might walk like Jesus did and become more sensitive to your presence. Father, help me to be more aware of the angelic realm around me as well as more aware of the presence of the Holy Spirit in my life. And most of all help me to know you more, in Jesus' name.

ACTIVATING YOUR SPIRITUAL SENSE OF SMELL

ow let's talk about the sense of smell. I have been in many revival meetings where God has opened up people's senses of smell. Many testimonies report people smelling supernatural fragrances or aromas from God in meetings, in times of prayer or worship, in their homes, or church meetings. I believe that at times, God will release signs and wonders to His people to get their attention or to relay a message to them. What I want to do is demystify the things of the supernatural and bring some understanding to some of the more unusual manifestations of God's spirit so that people won't worship a sign or conversely, miss what God is communicating to His people when He manifests the unusual.

I believe that often when people begin to smell supernatural fragrances, God is trying to get their attention in order to give them a message or direction in life.

I remember one time while ministering in a meeting in northern California when God opened up the sense of smell to almost everyone in a church that I ministered in. It happened right after the pastor called me up to speak for the evening meeting. As I stepped up to the pulpit, before I could introduce my self and start that night's message, the whole room was filled with the overwhelming smell of wine. I can still remember the look of surprise on some of the people's faces as it happened. This overwhelming fragrance of wine in the room went on for a long time.

That night, I was set on preaching a message on the fire of God and repentance. It was going to be one of those sobering words of repentance and no compromise. Then all of a sudden the Holy Spirit spoke to me just as the room was filled with wonder at this strange sign that God was manifesting. I was shocked at what He said to me. He said, "Son, I don't want you to preach on repentance and fire. I want to have a party with my people tonight and deliver and heal them through joy. Release the new wine of my presence."

As I heard this, I realized that God was trying to get my attention through that smell of wine. So I ended up changing my message and preached on the Joy of the Lord and the new wine of heaven. As I did, the presence of God overwhelmed many people. And many fell out of their seats in the joy of the Lord. Instead of having a repentance service, we had a party. It was one of the best meetings I had ever had. Many were healed and others were delivered from years of depression.

The Lord had me preach on Proverb 17:22 that talks about how laughter does the body good like medicine - *A joyful heart is good medicine, but a broken spirit dries up the bones.*

I was so glad that the Lord released this sign to us and opened our sense of smell in the meeting to give us direction to what His plan was for the meeting instead of mine. Signs and wonders are given to lead us in a direction. In this case, the sign of the fragrance of wine ushered in a mighty anointing of healing and refreshing which I might have missed if God would not have brought the supernatural direction of the fragrance of God.

I remember the first time I ever had an encounter with God when He first opened up my spiritual sense of smell. I was in Nashville, Tennessee, hanging out in this back room full of people at a big prophetic conference were Bob Jones was speaking. It was a real honor for me to be there, as Bob is known as one of the fathering prophets of our generation. He is one who was known for his incredible prophetic gifting as well as his humorist country personality. The man was extremely prophetic and totally unpredictable in what he might say or do.

This was the first time of many that I had been around Bob. One of my close friends named Jeff Jansen had invited me to come and meet Bob in the "green room" of his conference. There were around 30 or so people in this room and people were having a good time fellowshipping and hanging out. As we were all hanging out I noticed that people began to line up and get prayer from Bob. So I figured I would go to the end of the line and join in.

As Bob began praying for people He would prophesy over some as he went. I remember him getting to the guy next to me and thinking hopefully he will give me a word too. When Bob got done praying for the guy next to me he did something I never thought would happen. He looked me right in the eyes and said, "Sit down boy the anointing is gone." Then he turned around leaving me there feeling stupid for even trying to get prayer and went and sat down at a table next to the only door out of the room we were all in.

Talk about awkward. I felt like an idiot and just wanted to leave. I could hear others laughing in the room at what happened. After about 10 minuets or so, I decided to get up and leave. Then again the unexpected happened. As I reached for the door to leave Bob shouted out in front of everyone, "Come here boy; the anointing is back".

Then he grabbed me by the hand and said to me, "Do you smell that"?

Talk about random.

He went on again and said, "Come on boy sniff. Can you smell that?"

As he said this I began to sniff and didn't smell a thing, so I answered him, "Nope".

Then he said, "Come on boy. You're dull. Sniff again."

So I sniffed one more time and all of a sudden, I began to smell a Beautiful fragrance and I told Bob that I could smell it.

Then he went on to say, "Yep, you're a sweet smelling stench in your Father's nostrils. That's the fragrance of your intimacy and prayers rising to the Father in heaven. Then he said to me, "It's 1 Corinthians 2:14, which says *now thanks be to God who always causes us to triumph in Christ Jesus and through us releases the fragrance of Christ among the lost*".

Then, he prayed for me to receive impartation, encouraged me in my calling as an evangelist and told me that I was to release the fragrance of God's goodness and love to the lost people in the world who didn't know Him.

After that happened, everyone went from laughing at me to telling me how blessed I was to have received a prophetic word and impartation from Bob. Through this funny experience and through the scripture Bob shared with me out of 1 Corinthians 2:14 I realized that when Christ walks in a room there is a sweet smelling fragrance or aroma that comes in the room with Him. I believe that at times when the sign of the fragrance of God comes it can be that Jesus has stepped into the midst of His people and that the Holy Spirit has opened our sense of smell so that we know He is in the room. Other times, I believe that the fragrance could be from an angel sent from the very presence of the King to bring a message or minister God's love and presence to his people and since that angel had spent time in the very manifest presence of Jesus himself, the fragrance of the Lord rubbed off on the angel and he carried it into our realm.

I believe that just as Bob had prophesied that there was a fragrance coming from my life that was a sweet and pleasing aroma to my Father (which was a sign of my intimacy with God), that we can carry the fragrance of Jesus on our lives if we spend enough time in the presence of Jesus. The more time you spend with God, the more He begins to rub off on you. That's why Paul said in 1 Corinthians 2:14, *Now thanks be to God who always causes us to triumph in Christ and through us releases the fragrance of Christ amongst the lost.*

Have you ever smelled the scent of roses when none were in the room? Or the smell of wine? The fragrance of Christ wafting by you when you are at home alone? The scent of His presence is a wonderful gift in the moment. Sometimes He leaves the residue of heaven in a room for a specific purpose. Sometimes just to let you know that He is with you. Ask Him to activate your spiritual sense of smell so you can discern His presence more easily.

An empowerment prayer to get you there:

Lord, I pray that you would open my sense of smell in the spirit, that I might know you more and that I might be more aware of your presence. Lord, lead me into greater intimacy with You so that I smell and carry the fragrance of Christ among the lost, in Jesus' name.

ACTIVATING YOUR SPIRITUAL SENSE OF SIGHT

Now lets talk about seeing in the spirit. This is one of my favorite subjects to teach about when it comes to the five senses of the spirit. I believe that this is one of the most vital of the five senses. In John 5:19, Jesus said that He only did what he saw his Father doing in heaven and did in like manner. I believe that God wants to open up our eyes in the spirit and give us visionary encounters with him so we can know him more, as well as partner with Him in the spirit, to accomplish His will in the earth. The Bible is full of hundreds of testimonies about people who had God open up their spiritual sense of sight through supernatural encounters with Him in dreams and visions.

Acts 2:17-19 tells us that in our day God is pouring out His Spirit on all flesh and opening up heaven to release to the world dreams and visionary encounters. Lets take a look at this portion of scripture and we will find that not only does God want to open up His sons' and daughters' spiritual sense of sight but He wants to open up the whole world's sense of sight in order to reach them! Lets look a little deeper.

> *And it shall come to pass that in the last days, says God, That I will pour out my Spirit on all flesh; Your sons and your daughters shall prophesy, Your young men shall see visions, Your old men shall dream dreams. And on my Menservants and on My maidservants I will pour out My Spirit in those days; And they shall prophesy.*

It is funny to see in this portion of scripture that the first people who God pours out His spirit on is not limited to just Christians. He pours it out on the whole world. In fact, the Christians are the second mentioned group in this scripture. God said that He would pour out His spirit on ALL FLESH. That tells me that God wants to open people's eyes to His goodness and love and cause them, probably through visions and dreams, to know Him.

I have several friends from Indonesia who are leading powerful movements for God and their testimony about salvation is not that a man shared the Gospel with them, but that Jesus appeared to them personally in a dream or a vision. One of my friends in Indonesia used to be a powerful leader in the Muslim movement. Jesus appeared to him in a dream and told him that He loved him and that He was the only true God. As a result, the man got saved and has led thousands of other Muslims to the Lord. He now pastors a church of over 10,000, on-fire Christians in the biggest Muslim nation in the world.

The Bible is full of stories like this. Paul the apostle had a similar kind of thing happen to him. He was the main guy who was persecuting the early church after Christ had died and rose from the dead. Paul, known as Saul at that time, had authority from the religious church to kill those who had been following Christ. Suddenly, he had a life-changing encounter with God where his spiritual sense of sight was opened. A blinding light came out of heaven as he heard the audible voice of God change his life and it led him to understanding salvation in Christ (see Acts 8:19). After Paul was saved and fully launched into his ministry, spiritual sight was of the utmost importance and value to him. Not only was he a man known to have a powerful Apostleship but he also had genuine encounters with God that made him who he was. Paul was so different then all of the other Apostles. He went from being the greatest enemy and threat to the early church to the most powerful Apostle. Paul's testimony is much different then all of the other Apostles. Even though Paul did not travel one day with Jesus while he was in his earthly ministry, Paul accomplished more then any of the other Apostles who had traveled with Him. He ended up planting more churches, saving more people, and writing more of the New Testament then any of the others.

What made Paul's testimony different was that God taught him in the backside of the desert by opening his spiritual sense of sight and leading him through dreams, visions, and revelation (see Galatians 1:11-12). Paul was a "new breed" Apostle who would be taught by God Himself. Paul was fully walking and being led by supernatural encounters given by God. Paul, being one of the most powerful prophetic ministries in the Bible, actually taught about how God wanted to open up our eyes in the spirit in the book of Ephesians 1:15-19.

He prayed for the church (in Ephesians 1:15-19) that God the Father would give the people of that church a *Spirit of Wisdom and Revelation* in the knowledge of Him and that the *eyes of their understanding* would be opened that they might see into the spirit world. I believe that we can learn from Paul's teaching in order to understand how to position ourselves to receive spiritual sight. Lets take a closer look at Ephesians 1:15-19:

> *Therefore I also, after I heard of your faith in the Lord Jesus and your love for all the saints, do not cease to give thanks for you, making mention of you in my prayers: that the God of our Lord Jesus Christ, the Father of glory, may give to you the spirit of wisdom and revelation in the knowledge of Him, the eyes of your understanding being enlightened; that you may know what is the hope of His calling, what are the riches of the glory of His inheritance in the saints.*

The first thing I want to point out about the *Spirit of Wisdom and Revelation*, will be that God wants to anoint you to know him more. In Ephesians 1:17, Paul is praying that the Father of Glory would give unto the church (you and me) a *Spirit of Wisdom and Revelation* in the knowledge of Him. You see - it's all about knowing Him. The number one reason why God wants to open up your eyes in the spirit and give you a Spirit of Wisdom and Revelation is so that you will know Him more. The word Knowledge from the text above in the

Greek means, "to know the precise and correct knowledge of who God is." You see, God the Father is raising up a Kingdom of sons and daughters who will know their Father in heaven, and out of that place of authority, they will administrate his kingdom in the earth.

The second thing that I want to point out is that God wants to begin to open your eyes to see in the spirit for the purpose of revealing to you your calling and destiny, as well as his future plans for his kingdom purposes in the earth. In Ephesians 1:18 it says that *the eyes of your understanding being enlightened; that you may know what is the hope of His calling, what are the riches of the glory of His inheritance in the saints.* In this part of the scripture, Paul is praying that we would have the eyes of our understanding enlightened so that we would know the hope of Jesus' calling, and His inheritance in the saints. You see, when we as a church begin to see Jesus' calling, and the purpose for which he came, we begin to understand our calling and our purpose for which we are here.

God wants the eyes of our understanding to be enlightened. That phrase to have *the eyes of our understanding enlightened* means in the Greek language, to have the eyes of our hearts flooded with revelatory light. When you begin to tap into the spirit of wisdom and revelation, and the eyes of your heart begin to be flooded with revelatory light, you will begin to have dreams, visions, and supernatural encounters with God. These revelatory experiences are given in order to reveal to you the plans of God in the earth. God sent Jesus as a model for us to know how we should walk as the sons and daughters of the Most High God. Jesus never did a thing unless he first saw what his Father in heaven was doing (see John 5:19). God clearly wants us to see and understand the calling of Jesus, because when we do - we know who we are. And when we can clearly see what our Papa is doing, we can do great exploits for him.

After God began to open this revelation up to me, I began to make this portion of scripture personal, applying it to myself in prayer. I believe that there is power in praying scripture. We need to began to pray Eph 1:17-19 over ourselves. I just began to pray that scripture and put my name in it, praying for myself something like this: "Lord I am asking you to give me a Spirit of Wisdom. Give me a Spirit of Wisdom and Revelation in the knowledge of you. Open up my sense of sight and enlighten the eyes of my heart, God, that I might know Your calling in my life, that I might know the inheritance that You have for your son and for me."

I began to pray that every night before I went to sleep and you know what began to happen? I began having dreams, visions, and encounters with God. It wasn't a religious thing to me to pray that same prayer over and over again. I meant it with all my heart when I prayed this to God. What I was really saying was, "God I really want to know you."

One of the greatest things we can do to boost our spiritual sight is to read the Word. The Word of God will bring an impartation or framework to you so you can see. If you want to see heaven then start reading about heaven in the Bible. Read Revelation chapter 4 and 5 over and over again and ask God to open your sense of sight and to release to you the

Spirit of Wisdom and Revelation and watch what happens.

I remember when I first started really seeing angels in the spirit the Lord challenged me to read the Word. I was crying out day and night to see more in the Angelic realm and God kept telling me "Son if you want to see the angelic then study out the angels in the Bible." So, I started to look up every story about the angelic realm I could find in the book. I began to realize that in some portions of scriptures, there were many descriptions of what angels looked like and I began to learn by the word of God what their functions were. As God saw that I was a good steward of the Word He began to open my eyes in the spirit. I began to have encounters with the angelic realm. God started teaching me how to work with the angelic realm to see heaven invade earth. Still, to this day, seeing in the spirit and working with the angelic realm is one of the greatest keys that have enabled me to do what I do in ministry with God.

When God begins to show you things in the spirit its always for a purpose. I believe that God wants to open up your eyes to see so that He can show you what his game plan is for your life and for ministry. Often times in our healing meetings I will see the angelic and they come into the meetings like shafts of light. Usually what I do when I see these beings is ask God for words of knowledge for healing and then stand people right in the spot that I see the shafts of light. Most of the time people get healed. God wants us to be aware of what He wants to do in a city, state, region, or household. Sometimes, He will give us simple direction through a dream or vision to make a decree or pray about that direction and the results are huge when we follow through.

Obedience manifests the kingdom. God is going to rise up a generation who move in obedience just like Elijah, to do the same for the glory of God. Elijah walked in authority and power that was even demonstrated over the natural elements of the earth when he prophesied to King Ahab that there would be no rain except by his word. God is restoring the true prophetic to his church. So that when we speak the word of God it comes to pass.

Just a few months prior to the writing of this book, I was in Scotland doing a set of revival meetings in a city called Broxburn, just outside of Edinburgh. On the final night of the meetings, I had an open vision of a mighty gust of wind blowing throughout the land of Scotland and blowing a dark cloud away from the nation and into the sea. As the night came to an end, I felt the leading of the Holy Ghost to began to prophesy over the church and nation in this meeting. God told me to open wide my mouth and begin to speak and that as I did, He would fill it with His word for the people.

So I began telling everyone that God was releasing the winds of change in Scotland and that He was going to began to blow the darkness out of the nation to prepare the way for revival to be seen in there nation again. Then the Lord told me to tell the pastor that as a sign that this was the word of the Lord, he was to expect to see high winds in the natural after we left. These winds would be a sign of what God was doing in the spirit. After that, we left Scotland and went on to Mannheim, Germany. While we were in Mannheim I received an email from the pastor of the church in Scotland with a praise report. He wrote that after we left, Scotland experienced what the newspapers and media dubbed "The Storm of the Century". Scotland got hit with winds of over 114 mph - the strongest winds to hit the nation of Scotland in over a hundred years. Then the pastor went on to tell me that the winds were so strong that they even knocked down his back yard fence. God had confirmed his word about an impending revival with a sign in the natural. The winds were changing.

About a month after this email, I received another email from the same pastor praising God for breakthrough that had began to take place regarding revival and his church. He testified that before we had been with him and released the word about the winds of change and revival, he had a hard time gathering people for a meeting, or finding people who were hungry for revival in his region. He said that the first citywide meeting they held after we were with them was the best-attended event in years. God had brought forth a shift in both the attendance of his events as well as hunger in the land for a move of God's spirit.

Another reason why God wants to open up your sense of sight is because God wants to give us confidence. Something happens when you know who is for you rather then who is against you. I have been in many meetings in third world nations were it is not safe to preach the gospel. We have been through war zones and places were it's illegal to preach, places were people are being killed daily. I remember just recently, being in a very dangerous city in Peru. We were there to do a crusade and our contact brought to my attention just how dangerous it was for us to be in that place preaching. They told me our crusade was set up right in the middle of an area that was known as one of the most violent gang areas of Peru. They told us to make sure we kept a good watch on our team and make sure nothing happened to them.

I remember that night as the worship was going, God opened my spiritual sense of sight and I saw a huge angel of pure white light the size of a two-story building, appear right above the platform I was about to speak on. As I saw this, I was filled with boldness because I knew God was showing me that I didn't need to worry at all - heaven was backing me up. As God spoke this to me, I got up and spoke with supernatural boldness and power, and many gave their lives to Jesus that night and many radical miracles happened, too.

A similar thing happens in the book of 2 Kings when a large army shows up outside of Elisha's house to overtake him. His servant was scared to death about it. The young man runs into Elisha's presence and freaks out telling him about the great army. Elisha tells him not to worry because those that were with them were greater then those that were against them. As he speaks this he says a prayer for his servant and says, "Open his eyes Lord that he might see." The Lord honors the prayer and opens up his servant's sense of spiritual sight and the guy instantly starts seeing a sky filled with Angelic hosts riding on fiery Chariots in the sky. Like Elisha, he is no longer afraid (see 2 Kings 6:17).

God wants to open your eyes to see. He wants to show you

His plans and blueprints for your life. He wants to give you confidence in the fact that He has your back in all that you do. He wants to give you a Spirit of Wisdom and Revelation - and just like I talked about earlier, God wants you to begin to cry out and ask for it in prayer. Just like Elisha's servant had his eyes open by a simple prayer of faith I pray right now that God would open up your sense of sight in the spirit.

An empowerment prayer to get you there:

Lord, open up my sense of sight. Give me a Spirit of Wisdom and Revelation in the knowledge of you that I might know You more. Open the eyes of my heart and flood them with prophetic light that I might know Your plans and blueprint for my life, so that I might partner with You to see heaven invade earth, in Jesus' name.

ACTIVATING YOUR SPIRITUAL SENSE OF TASTE

Now let's talk about the sense of taste. The Bible is full of stories about God opening up people's senses of taste to the spirit of God. In Ezekiel 3:1-3, it tells us that God commissioned Ezekiel by giving him a scroll and telling him to eat that scroll. As he ate the scroll it was sweet like honey in his mouth and bitter in his stomach. Lets take a look at this scripture.

> *Then He said to me, "Son of man, eat what you find: eat this scroll, and go, speak to the house of Israel." So I opened my mouth, and He fed me this scroll. He said to me, "Son of man, feed your stomach and fill your body with this scroll which I am giving you." Then I ate it, and it was sweet as honey in my mouth.*

In this story, God opened up Ezekiel's sense of taste in the spirit and fed him a scroll. The end result of Ezekiel eating this scroll was that it tasted like honey in his mouth. Then,

He was commanded to go and speak the word of the Lord to all of Israel. You see, when God begins to fill you with His Word, it will become revelation in your mouth and you will have the ability to speak His inspired Word to others.

I have had times in our meetings, especially while preaching, where the Lord speaks to me and says to me, "Son, today I want to release scrolls of destiny to people like Ezekiel ate. Release them." There have been several times we have released prophetic teaching on the five senses of the Spirit and declared that God was opening up the sense of taste. Many individuals testified afterwards that God had open up their sense of taste and sight at the same time as they experienced God giving them a scroll in the spirit.

Everything God does is with a purpose. God's Word invites us to taste and see that He is good! When God does this with the individual, they usually see a life scripture and taste the taste of honey in their mouth. The end result is impartation. Often when people have these kinds of encounters like Ezekiel did, it is a form of commissioning and impartation to their lives to thrust them into a greater place of intimacy and destiny with God. If the early church was led and empowered by God giving them supernatural encounters then so should we be led and empowered in this way.

John also had a similar encounter to the one Ezekiel experienced in the book of Revelation 10:9-11. Here we read that an Angel handed John a book and told him to eat it. As John ate that book, it became sweet like honey in his mouth. He was then commanded to prophesy to people, nations and

Kings. This is the second time in scripture that you see the Lord open up someone's sense of taste and impartation is released to prophesy over kings, nations, and people.

I have tangibly tasted of a heavenly substance before. One day, one of my friends brought me some supernatural manna that came from heaven like the Bible talks about in the book of Exodus. He had been to a meeting with a man named Harold Byer. Harold was known to have had a ministry of signs, wonders, and miracles. Over 30 years ago, while Harold was driving around a milk truck and praying, the Lord visited him in a very supernatural way. He felt the presence of God come in a very unusual way and when he looked down at his Bible, he noticed that there was a white flakey bread-looking substance on his Bible covering the 60th chapter of Isaiah. The Lord spoke to him and told him it was manna.

This began to happen repeatedly and eventually it birthed his ministry. After this supernatural phenomenon begin to happen, hundreds and even thousands came to Harold to hear the word of the Lord. Many got touched and saved in his meetings. When Harold would preach on Isaiah 60, the supernatural manna would appear on his Bible during the meetings and God would instruct him to have the people take communion with the manna. I even heard about a time when Harold and a few other ministers were holding some meetings together. One of the other ministers realized that God had supernaturally transformed the water in a water bottle he had in his hotel room into wine. That night he went to the meeting with his water bottle. Harold had the manna show up, and they were able to take communion with the miraculous elements. The most amazing thing was that the manna only lasted to the very last person who was taking communion and that was it. I love that God already knows ahead of time how much to send before communion would start.

On other occasions God would give Harold manna while in prayer and Harold and his wife Kay would give the manna to people who were sick or dying from terminal illnesses. They would be healed as they ate the supernatural substance during communion. People who had cancer would eat the manna and instantly the cancer left their bodies. Divine healing happened as a result of the supernatural bread that was eaten.

This is Biblical! You can see this exact thing take place with Elijah in 1Kings 19:5-8. In this part of scriptures it tells us that Elijah is tired and weary from running from Jezebel after a mighty victory over the prophets of Baal on Mount Carmel. As he stopped to rest, he fell asleep under a broom tree. All of a sudden, an angel appears to him and wakes him up and gives him a jar of water to drink and a cake to eat. After Elijah eats the cake and drinks the water he begins to tap into a supernatural health and strength. The Bible tells us that he ran for 40 days and nights straight to the Mountain of the Lord and did not eat or drink along the way (see 1Kings 19:8). So, if an angel of the Lord would release a supernatural impartation to Elijah through the sense of taste and supernatural bread why would he not do it again in our day? Hebrews 13:8 tells us that God is the same today as yesterday and forever, and He never changes!

I have had many encounters in dreams or visions were God opened up my sense of taste and I have tasted things in the spirit. I remember one time, while waiting on God in prayer, I fell into a trance-vision and I found myself at this dinning table with Jesus. As I was in this experience, Jesus gave me a steak to eat. It sounds funny but it's the truth. This experience was very real to me. I could even taste the steak as I began to eat it. It was an amazing experience!

As I begin to eat this steak it was like all of my spiritual senses began to come alive, especially the sense of taste and touch. I was literally vibrating in the presence of God's spirit in this encounter. It was one of the strongest times of the manifest presence of God that I have ever experienced! After this encounter, I sought the Lord on the meaning of this strange visitation. As I did, He began to speak to me about the encounter being an encounter of Impartation and Commissioning. He said to me, "Son you just ate a steak of impartation and revelation."

I said to Him, "Where is that at in the Bible".

Then He answered, "Hebrews 5:14."

When I looked up what Hebrews 5:14 said I was amazed! It reads: *But solid food is for the mature, who because of practice have their senses trained to discern good and evil.*

Then the Lord began to speak to me more about this scripture as I studied it out. As I looked up the meaning of the word *food* I found that in the Greek, this word really meant strong meat! So the Lord showed me that I had partaken of the strong meat or steak of his Word. From that point on, I began to get so much revelation out of God's Word and my anointing to preach and teach the word went to a whole new level. Part of walking in revelation is the understanding of the gift of discernment. The gift of discernment often times works within visions and dreams – co-existing in the place where God speaks to us most clearly. What discernment does is open up the co-existing realm of the spirit to us. It is a gift that allows you to discern, or know, what is going on in the unseen world of the spirit - both in the heavenly realm as well as the demonic. I teach much more on this subject in my book *Activating your Dream Language* that is a part of this empowerment series.

An empowerment prayer to get you there:

Have you ever had God open your sense of taste in the Spirit? In his Word it says to taste and see that He is good! I believe that God wants to release encounters to us like Ezekiel. God wants to give us scrolls of destiny and commissioning.

So Lord, I pray that you would open up my sense of Taste that I would know you more. Release encounters to me; encounters like Ezekiel and Elijah had where I taste of your goodness in the spirit - in Jesus name!

ABOUT JERAME NELSON

Jerame Nelson is the founder of Living at His Feet Ministries. He is an author, as well as a well-known international conference speaker and a crusade revivalist to the nations. It's Jerame's passion to equip the body of Christ in the areas of hearing God's voice, as well as walking in the supernatural power of God in everyday life. Jerame and his wife, Miranda, live in San Diego, California, and work together in the ministry to change the lives of thousands through the Gospel of Jesus Christ.

PRODUCTS

Other products by Jerame include:

Manifesting God's Love through Signs, Wonders, and Miracles
(Destiny Image Publishers, 2010)

Burning Ones: Calling forth a Generation of Dread Champions
(Destiny Image Publishers, 2011)

Come into the Glory:
A Techno Experience

CONTACT

For more information on the ministry and writings of Jerame Nelson go to: www.livingathisfeet.org

Address:
      Living At His Feet Ministries
      591 Telegraph Canyon Rd. Suite 705
      Chula Vista, CA 91910

Email: admin@livingathisfeet.org
Follow Jerame Nelson on Twitter at: @jeramenelson

Living At His Feet
PUBLICATIONS

CPSIA information can be obtained at www.ICGtesting.com
Printed in the USA
BVOW031637111012

302577BV00001B/5/P